Pound a
Poem

Pound a Poem

**The winning entries from the National
Schools poetry competition**

Published by Metro Publishing
an imprint of John Blake Publishing Ltd
3 Bramber Court, 2 Bramber Road,
London W14 9PB, England

www.blake.co.uk

First published in hardback in 2007

ISBN 978 1 84454 436 3

British Library Cataloguing-in-Publication Data:

A catalogue record for this book is available from the British Library.

Design by www.envydesign.co.uk

Printed and bound in Great Britain by Cromwell Press Ltd

1 3 5 7 9 10 8 6 4 2

Illustrations by Myrna Sayers

Papers used by John Blake Publishing are natural, recyclable
products made from wood grown in sustainable forests.
The manufacturing processes conform to the environmental
regulations of the country of origin.

The Pears Foundation

**Pound a Poem is proudly sponsored by
The Pears Foundation**

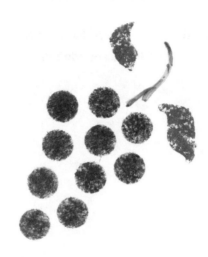

The Grape and Vine

by Celia Abrahams

There was a man
His name was Joe
He was my dad
I loved him so

Joe was a man
Of another time
His favourite fruit
Grew on the vine

This book I dedicate
To Joe …
And the Grape
The fruit that he loved so!

Edgar Allen Poetato

www.poundapoem.com

A Word About Pound a Poem

In 2005, Celia Abrahams, a dedicated supporter of Cancer Research UK, had an idea to do some fundraising around one of her loves – poetry. Celia gradually formed around her a team of volunteers, all experts in their field, and together they built the concept. The team wanted to craft something that would help to teach children about the importance of healthy eating and just how vital it is that we all try and eat five portions of fruit and vegetables every day. Poetry had always been at the heart of the concept and so it was decided that children would be asked to write a poem about fruit and vegetables; it was also a fantastic way of further engaging children with literacy. At the same time, the team wanted the children involved to recognise that they had the potential to help other children who sadly have been diagnosed with cancer and so Pound a Poem was born. Children were asked to pay £1 for every poem they entered into the competition. All of that money has been used specifically by Cancer Research UK to fund research into the cancers that affect children.

Pound a Poem was officially launched in September 2006 and has been in this, its first year, hugely successful. We have had over 20,000 entries from across the UK and the standard of poetry was incredibly high. We are proud to have had support from so many wonderful people, all listed in our acknowledgements, without whom we would not have been able to achieve such success.

We would like to thank all the schools that engaged with Pound a Poem 2006/2007. Congratulations to everyone that entered a poem into this year's competition. They were all wonderful. Thank you for raising vital funds for Cancer Research UK.

And from Cancer Research UK, thank you to Celia and the team for your passion and enthusiasm that made it all happen.

Acknowledgements
Thank you ...

So many people have been involved with Pound a Poem since its inception. We are incredibly grateful to you all. Without you, we would not be where we are today. Pound a Poem and Cancer Research UK would like to thank you for believing in the concept and for giving so much commitment and enthusiasm.

For your invaluable guidance and endorsement:
Department for Education and Skills, National Literacy Trust, Poetry Society, School Foods Trust, TeacherNet.

For your magnificent support, without which, much of Pound a Poem simply would not have happened:
John Blake Publishing, Espresso, Everyclick.com, Geronimo Communications, Hayward Design & Print, JazzyMedia Ltd., Louis Kennedy, Radio & TV Consultancy, Scholastic Publishing UK, Stokes PLC, SZ Education, Vocal Heroes Ltd , Simon Sharkey, David Lazaro, Moving Picture Company, Skarda Films, Sue Moles Editing.

For your fundamental support, time and expertise our very special thanks go to:
Adrian Hughes, Anastasia Scott, Andy Piddock, Andrew

Feldman, Anna Hilton, Ashley Tyas, Childs Hill School, David Jeffers, Ben Magahy, Elaine Davies, Edward Kerner, Eddie Hammerman, Jacqueline Fitzgerald, John Blake, Jonathan Harris CBE, John Goldfinger, Julie Randel, Justin Brukman, Lester Headley, Lisa Flanagan, Marc Lester, Martin Davidson, Michelle Signore, Mike Tiddy, Nicola Roberts, Petra Roach, Polly Gower, Richard Comline, Richard Gerver, Richard Essberger, Ro Jordan, Sue Breetzke, Sue Moles, Stephanie Moore, Laura and Russell Nathan, Tim North, Winton Rossiter, Natalie Morris, Rachel Zeitland, Charles Keidan, Pru Leith, Cyril Dennis MBE, Claire Dowse, Paul Ashford and Mohamed Mouzoun.

For your special support and all the time you have given us, thank you:
Annabel Karmel MBE, Danni Harmer, Dick and Dom, Gino D'Acampo, Jacqueline Wilson, James Campbell, Kim Britten, Maureen Lipman, Tracy-Ann Oberman, Richard Phillips, Nikki Woolf, Trevor Pears, Charles Keidan, Grant Morgan and Karen Harris.

To all those who kindly got us up and running:
Louis Kennedy, Berry World Ltd, United Biscuits, Greencore, Steiner, Nick Finegold, David and Sandra Chester, David Alexander, Michael and Claire Abrahams.

To the Production Team, who have been such a driving force behind Pound a Poem:

Celia Abrahams, Ruth Abrahams, David Alexander, Michele Bentata, Dominic Cook, Paul Corren, Judy Dewinter, Jayne Franklin, Gillian Goldberg, Jonathan Harris CBE , Melanie Jawett, Geraldine Krieger, Grainne Lamphee, Ruth Mowlem, Richard Phillips, Myrna Sayers, Nikki Woolf.

Huge thanks to all the judges in the competition who had the most enjoyable, but also the most difficult job of reading all the poems and deciding the winners:

Annabel Karmel, Ann Wittekind, Carol Pesskin, Carolyn Askar, Dominic Wood, Jacqueline Wilson, James Campbell, Jane Epstein, Jennifer Sanford , Julie Randles , Juliet Lewin, Penny Telfer and Richard Phillips.

To Anthony, who has put up with so much.
To Katie, who got the wheels in motion.
Thank you both.

10 DOWNING STREET
LONDON SW1A 2AA

THE PRIME MINISTER

I am delighted to give my personal support to Cancer Research UK's "Pound a Poem" competition.

It's a fantastic initiative which will not only raise money for cancer research but will also encourage young people to write and also to think about what they can do to stay healthy throughout their lives. That's a hat-trick of very worthwhile achievements for just one competition.

So my congratulations to everyone behind the "Pound a Poem" competition – and best of luck to all the children taking part. It's a great idea and deserves widespread support.

Tony Blair

June 2006

Rt Hon DAVID CAMERON MP

HOUSE OF COMMONS
LONDON SW1A 0AA

LEADER OF THE OPPOSITION

June 2006

"Pound a Poem"

I am delighted to welcome this competition in aid of Cancer Research UK, and would encourage as many young people as possible to enter.

Poems can both amuse and stir the imagination. I am sure once this collection is assembled it will encourage more to put pen to paper in future. And, above all, everyone who contributes will be helping to raise valuable funds in the fight against cancer.

We all have a shared responsibility for our shared future. Individuals, families, government, business, and voluntary organisations all have a vital role to play in making our country a better place to live for everyone. Fundraising initiatives like the "Pound a Poem" competition are examples of these principles being put into practice.

It's great that people from so many different walks of life have already submitted poems. I am sure that children from across the country will now be encouraged to follow suit.

I would like to wish "good luck" to everyone who enters.

David Cameron

THE RT. HON. SIR MENZIES CAMPBELL C.B.E. Q.C. M.P.

HOUSE OF COMMONS
LONDON SW1A 0AA

September 2006

I am delighted to lend my support to Cancer Research UK's 'Pound a Poem' competition. This is fantastic way of educating children about the importance of healthy eating and literacy, while also raising money for children who have been affected by cancer

I wish Cancer Research UK every success for this competition and the future.

Sir Menzies Campbell

The Poems

A Vegetable Variety and Fabulous Fruits

Vitamins A, B and C,
Eating luscious vegetables breakfast, lunch and tea,
Gorgeous and succulent, sour and bitter.
Even old E numbers thrown out with the litter,
The aroma of the dreamy juices,
And even ugly sprouts may have their uses.
Blissful blends of organic green growth,
Lavish ranges pledge your personal oath,
Eat vegetables, grow up strong, make your life fun,
Joyous and long.

Fabulous fruit juicy and sweet,
Refresh your taste buds, a real treat,
Undeniable pleasure to be found,
Irresistible satisfaction can come from the ground,
Torrents of juice held in the skin, the fierce taste
rollercoaster of fabulous fruit.

Sean Jarvis • Year 6
Yarm Primary School

3

James Campbell

Children's Comedian

Courgettes

If a cigarette is a small cigar
And a corvette is a fast and very large car,
Is a courgette a tiny little courge?
What shape would that be and what sort of size?
And what's a courge anyway?
Please advise.

Dom Wood

Dick and Dom

Television Presenters

Poem

There once was a veggi called Dom
Who thought eating meat was so wrong.
He ate all his greens,
With lentils and beans
And then wrote this wonderful song.

There once was a fella called Dick
Who was feeling incredibly sick,
He ate a red pepper
That made him feel better
So he said 'That's done the trick'

Eat Your Beans

Eat your beans!
Eat your beans!

So many to choose from, but they're not all green.

Broad beans, string beans, baked beans and soya,
French beans, kidney beans, black eyed beans and lima.

Put them in a salad, spoon them from a pot,
Add them to a tasty soup and cook them nice and hot.

Mmmmmmmm!

Munch your beans!
Chomp your beans!

Get them in your tummy by any means!

Runner beans, jumping beans and beans from Mexico,
Cocoa beans, mung beans and beans called haricot.

Boil them in a saucepan, bake them in a dish,
Serve them up with chicken or with a juicy fish.

Yummy!

The whole world is full of beans
So next time remember
EAT YOUR BEANS!!!!!

Isabel Ann Cottis • Year 5
Blackheath High School
London

Brian Croucher

Actor

Me

I once was an apple
I wanted to be a bean
Someone said you are a carrot
All I want to be is Me!!!

My Healthy Body

Orange, orange
Beautiful and round,
Helps my body
Stay healthy and sound.

Apple, apple
Beautiful and green,
Helps my teeth
Stay sparkling and clean.

Carrot, carrot
Beautiful and long,
Makes my eyes stay
Super strong.

Broccoli, broccoli
Beautiful like a tree,
Helps me stay
Illness free.

Holly Graveney • Year 3
Orchard House School
London

Exotic Banana

My exotic banana comes off the ship still
Green, bitter and unripe.
You are like a crescent shaped moon.

Sitting in my fruit bowl,
You have had a long journey from the
plantations of Jamaica.

I peel off your skin and what do I find?
A curvy bent, slippery, soft and spotted
Fawn coloured banana.
Messily you stick to my baby sister's
fingers, face and hair.

Your sweet aroma calls to my tummy soon
To be filled with a delicious treat.

Yolanda Piotrowicz • Year 4
Chetham's School of Music
Manchester

Fabulous Food!

When I'm hungry I like to eat
Food that keeps me 'on my feet'
Food that helps me run about
Helps me skip and jump and shout!

Things like carrots, apples, pears
Things that help me run upstairs!
Milk and cheese and yoghurts too
Helps my brain think problems through!

Healthy smoothies made at school
Helped me learn the 'golden rule'
GOOD FOOD WILL HELP KEEP US FIT
And I can't get enough of it!

Phebe • Year 3
Blackheath High School
London

Rob Bennet

Sports Commentator

The Mushroom and the Onion

The mushroom wears a rounded cap
That sits upon his head
He's short and stubby, and very tasty
With a piece of bread

His friend the onion makes you cry
When he gets undressed
He's very strong and a little smelly
And has a lot of zest

Fruit And Veg Are Good For You

Fruit and veg are good for you,
Your mother, brother, sister too,
Eat five a day the experts say,
You'd better get started right away!

Apple, carrot, peach or pear,
Hand them round there's loads to share,
Fruit and veg tasty and sweet,
Give them a try, you'll have a treat!

Hannah Thomas • Year 3
Cymer Afan Primary
Port Talbot

Tracy-Ann Oberman
Actor

Kiwi and Mango

I come from New Zealand,
They call me a Kiwi,
I'm thick skinned and really quite green.
I mix well with mango,
As we like to tango,
And dance a fandango,
In fruit salads –
You know what I mean!

Fruit and Veg!

They live in my fridge,
They sit on my table,
I eat five a day 'if I'm able!'

Strawberries and sweetcorn,
They're my favourites,
Cabbage and sprouts,
'Eat them up!' my mum shouts!

Skinned and peeled,
Mashed and beaten.
Poor old fruit and veg,
Sewn and grown to be eaten.

Peas are odd, they grow in a pod!
Grapes grow on a vine and get turned into wine,
Bananas get bent, before they are sent,
Cauliflower, 'urgh!' I gave that up for lent.

Fresh, frozen, canned and dried,
Boiled, steamed, baked and fried,
Love them or hate them,
Don't call them till you've tried.

Bethany Delvard • Year 4
St Brendan's RC School
Bolton

Libby Purves

Author

Swede

If a Swede
Is what you really need
You don't want a turnip
To turn up!

Michael Morpugo

Author and Former Children's Laureate

Bananas for Befores

Bananas for befores
Melons for mains
And apples for afters
That way I'll
Last a little longer
Laugh a little louder
And live a little ever

By then I'll
Be a very old
And wrinkly and a falling-apart ruin
But hey, I'll be healthy and wonderfully wise

So wise, I'll go on having
Bananas for befores
And so on for a little ever
But I'll leave writing poetry
To those that can do it properly!

Fruit and Veg!

Come on parents
Don't be mean,
Give us some food
That's healthy and green.

Burgers and chips
May be a hoot,
But we want a change
Like veggies and fruit.

There is not a taste
That can compare,
To a ripe and juicy
Conference pear.

Here is a thought
And it's the real deal,
Two kinds of veg
In every meal.

If you want us to be jolly
Give us cabbage
Give us sprouts
Give us cauli.

Without fruit and veg
I'd like to mention,
You might not live
To enjoy your pension.

Rhiannon Weeks • Year 6
St Mary's RC School
Denton

23

Fruit Divine

The physalis is the morning sun,
rising from its veined cocoon.
Its colour is a mellowed red,
I sniff its lush perfume.
As I place its tender skin on my tongue,
I loll it round my teeth.
Then I bite into its seedy hyde,
And the pulpy sugar beneath.

The dragon fruit is violent green,
Tinged with a luminous pink.
And inside is grey and especially seedy,
with a very bland taste, I think.
Compared with a juicy tender melon,
It's not something I would call good.
However, I certainly must agree,
It can still be called a fruit.

The pomegranate is a furnace red,
Streaked with a blinding white.
The inside is full of crunchy seeds,
that you pick up and slowly bite.

The problem is there's never enough,
From the base of the fruit to the vine.
Berries to oranges, bananas and grapes,
Fruit is always divine!

Max Wolffe • Year 4
George Watson's College
Edinburgh

Fruit 'n' Veg

Apples, bananas, carrots and peas,
Sweetcorn and strawberries, are the bees knees.
Eat these foods daily and you will be
Strong and healthy, just like me.

George Stevens • Year 3
Town Junior School
West Midlands

Gino D'Acampo
Chef

Sun-dried and Roasted

To make a sauce
You must of course
Use tomatoes that dry in the sun,
Basil drizzled with oil
Just fit for a royal
Add some capers one by one.

A red pepper to roast
With crushed garlic on toast
And an olive or two on the side
Is so very delicious
Please don't be suspicious
These can be eaten with relish and pride.

Fruits of our Planet

Oranges are tasty, yummy and sweet.
Apples go crunch and are very good to eat.
Bananas are soft, squishy and good,
Full of potassium, they're a very healthy food.
Grapes are small but juicy and yummy,
I wish I had some now to fill up my tummy.
The fruits of our planet cultivated or wild.
Five portions makes a happy and healthy child.

Frankie McFadden • Year 6
St Charles Primary
Glasgow

Charles Ghinga

Poet

Quiet Diet

Mom has found the
perfect diet
All she wants
Is peas and quiet

Gathering Apples

A ripe Autumn sun,
Shines down upon the orchard,
Where five children,
Each carrying a woven basket,
Are gathering apples.
The ripest, juiciest apples,
Dangle from the highest of branches.
One boy
Scrambles up the gnarled trunk,
Ignoring the angry cries coming
From his worried mother,
Higher he climbs,
Until he is face to face,
With a large, crimson apple.
He stares at it in awe,
Before plucking it from its branch.

Hester Wolton • Year 6
Orchard House School
London

Will Carling OBE
Former England Rugby Player

Scrummy

The centre of a cabbage
Is really very scrummy
You can try a red or green one
They're tasty and they're yummy

It could also be a penalty
Not to choose a kale
Just convert it into coleslaw
It's a winner without fail

Grandad Phil's Allotment

(To be sung to the tune of 'Oh I do like to be
beside the seaside')

Oh I do like to dig Grandad's Allotment
It's got lots of veg I love to eat
Oh I do like to plant the seeds and watch them grow
I'll get rid of weeds with my trowel and hoe

Oh I do like to put my Wellie boots on
And plant lots of parsnips for my tea
There's enormous runner beans
And pumpkins for Halloween
Grandad's allotment – it is supreme

Oh I do like to see the cauli-flowering
The carrots will help my eyes to see
Oh I do like to dig potatoes big and white
I could eat roasted veggies every single night

Oh I do like tomatoes, peas and cabbage
And sweetcorn's as tasty as can be
Grandad's strawberries are sweet
They're the nicest things to eat
So my nan makes jam, 'specially for me!

Oliver Moss • Year 6
Sharmans Cross Junior School, Solihull

Green Veg Mad

I love cabbage
I love beans
I'll eat anything
As long as it's greens

I want broccoli
I want sprouts
If I don't get my greens
I'll scream and shout!

Eat more cucumber
Eat more kale
If you don't eat your greens
You'll look a bit pale

I like lettuce
I like peas
Ooh what's that
Pass the artichoke please!

Maximilian Bennett • Year 4
Ibstock Place School
London

Twiggy
Model

HotchPotch

Tomatoes are tasty
Watercress is feisty
In a favourite salad of mine
Grapefruits are fine
Guavas a should
Yams are scrumptiously good

Carolyn Askar
Poet

Crazy Colours

Green grow the carrots oh –
that's just the way they sprout,
the orange roots hide underground
until I pull 'em out.

Oranges aren't yellow
that's what you're going to say –
but I'm sure I saw some big ones
just the other day –
grapefruits, right!
well, they all keep colds away.

Grapes are red and white
or black like bramble berries,
while berries (rasp and straw)
are red - like peppers HOT
if you like to eat 'em raw,
follow with a cool paw-paw!

Leaves (that keep me healthy)
can be purple, green or cream
(though not when they turn slimey brown
like something in a stream)
so I eat 'em quick, nice and crisp,
or lightly cooked in steam.

This is the brightly coloured food
I like to eat each day,
and I can't think of a single fruit,
or veg, that's simply grey.

Can you??

In the Hedge

I like fruit
I like veg
I like picking berries
from my hedge.

Some are red
Some are blue
Most of them
are good for you.

I eat fruit
five times a day
Which helps me work hard,
think and play.

I'm glad I like fruit
I'm glad I like veg
And I'm glad
I can pick berries
Free from my hedge.

Aaron Duthie • Year 4
Llanmdrlais Primary
Swansea

David Seaman MBE

Former England Goalkeeper

They're Crispy

They're crispy
They're spicy
Where do they come from?
With bhajis and puris
And a big poppadom
With chutney and yogurt
And cucumber too
Is it madras or murgha or vindaloo?

Indigo Jam

At the bottom of my garden there is a prickly bramble
bush heavy with blackberries.

After picking them, my hands look like an ink cartridge
has exploded all over them.

I pile the small shiny berries into a saucepan and it
reminds me of the night sky.

The purply-black bubbling jam sends delicious,
scrumptious smells around the kitchen making me
feel hungry.

I use the velvety jam to fill a Victoria sponge

And enjoy!

Reece • Year 5
Arunside School
West Sussex

40

Keep a Healthy Diet

We are told by doctors to watch what we eat
To keep our bodies trim and neat
To eat five portions of fruit and veg
On a daily basis we make that pledge
Potatoes, greens, carrots and beans
Will help you in your early teens.
Eat plenty of fruit such as apples and pears
And enjoy good health in the coming years
So take the tip and watch your weight
Don't eat junk food and so tempt fate.

Cameron Ryan • Year 4
St Francis Catholic School
Kent

Annabel Karmel MBE

Children's Food and Nutrition Writer

Baby Veggies

There are baby carrots
and baby courgettes
and baby corn on the cob
you can make a puree
or make a mash
They're delicious whatever
the job.

There are baby mushrooms
and baby shallots
and baby leeks as well,
you can steam them together
or put in a bake
they could stop your baby yell!

Lemon

On the outside it's round and golden, a sun perfect
for a hot summer's day,

On the inside it's a beautiful blossoming sunflower.

It smells of a newborn baby, sweet and innocent,

It tastes like a person whose heart has no room
for kindness.

Inside it's a smooth and slippery someone who
you dare not trust,

Outside it's hard and rumpled like a giant's leather boot.

Ella Minson • Year 6
Bryn Coch, Wales

Lime

A small green sphere,
The fresh open sea,
The ripples of the water,
A leaf on a blooming flower,
The fresh clean wind in the air,
Soft wet silk,
Bitter hard boiled sweets,
One bite and your tongue will tingle and quiver!

Naomi Watters • Year 5
Whitehouse Primary School
Newtownabbey

Jackie Kay

Author

Grandpa's Soup

No one makes soup like Grandpa's,
With its diced carrots the perfect size
And its diced potatoes the perfect size
And its wee soft bits –
What are their names?
And its big bit of hough,
Which rhymes with loch, floating
Like a rich island in the middle of the soup sea.
I say, Grandpa, Grandpa, your soup is the best soup
in the whole world.
And Grandpa says, Och,
Which rhymes with hough and loch,
Och, don't be daft,
Because he is shy about his soup, my Grandpa.
He knows I will grow up and pine for it.
I will fall ill and desperately need it.
I will long for it my whole life after he is gone.
Every soup will become sad and wrong after he is gone.
He knows when I'm older I will avoid soup altogether.
Oh Grandpa, Grandpa, why is your soup so glorious? I say
Tucking into my fourth bowl in a day.
Barley! That's the name of the wee soft bits. Barley.

If I Were A... I Would

If I were a cherry I would hold on to the wet,
brown branch.
If I were a lemon I would peel off my bumpy skin to catch
the blinding sunlight.
If I were a banana I would stretch out wide to find a little
beetle crawling over my yellow skin.
If I were a cabbage I would open wide my delicate,
green face.
If I were a strawberry I would throw out my black
pips onto the fields.

Carl • Year 4
Arunside School
Horsham

48

Lunch! Lunch! Lunch!

I'm a big banana sitting on a tree
Along comes a farmer – he's looking up at me.

'You look tasty, you look ripe.
You look lovely – just my type.'

Ow! He's pulling on my friends hanging on my bunch
And who's that little boy yelling
Lunch, lunch, lunch!!!

Ouch he's pulling harder, hard as can be
Oh dear! Oh no! He's pulling down me.

He's pulled off my yellow skin – oh what a disgrace!
The little boy has slipped on it and fallen on his face!

Verity Foster • Year 4
Royal Junior School
Surrey

More Vegetables

One day whilst walking in the garden
I thought I heard 'I beg your pardon.'
It made me jump, I looked around
And sitting there upon the ground
Alone and looking sleek and green
The biggest cabbage that I've seen.

It said to me, 'I'm glad you looked
Because it's time that I was cooked.
Run in the house and tell your Mummy
I'm ready now to fill a tummy.
Potatoes, sprouts and two nice chops
We'll make a meal that is the tops.'

It's funny how the things one sees
Like carrots, beans and fresh green peas
Remind us that we have to eat,
How nice they taste when served with meat
And now you really must admit
It's vegetables that keep you fit.

Emma Evans • Year 4
Walmley Junior School
West Midlands

Jason Leonard
Ex-England Rugby Player

Potato

You can boil it
You can roast it
You can buy it in a packet
You can fry it
You can mash it
It even wears a jacket.

There Are Monsters In
My Fruit Bowl

There's a large scarred, round face,
Staring at me,
Rough orange wrinkles,
and scary to see.

There's a moon shaped banana,
with a black snouty nose,
and muddy brown spots
from his head to his toes.

There are ruby red spheres
With rosy red cheeks,
Chattering, nattering
with their stalk pointy beaks.

There are oval green goblins
tied up in a rope,
trapped by the mango
they've given up hope.

Rosie Scott • Year 3
St Francis College
Letchworth Garden City
Herts

Mum Knows Best

My mum told me to eat my fruit and veg.
I ignored her because I thought that was best.
She kept going on and on telling me to eat,
A juicy orange for a treat.
Instead I opened the cupboard door
Grabbed some sweets and sat on the floor.

One day it went bad.
My teeth were hurting and I was sad.
I sat on the dentist chair,
I closed my eyes and grabbed my hair.
I sat back and opened my mouth wide,
It twizzled and twizzled as it went inside.

Now I eat my fruit and veg,
Because mum knows best.

Corey Sykes • Year 4
Heathcoat Primary,
Devon

Peas

Peas are green
Peas are sweet
Peas are healthy
Peas are a treat

Peas in soup
Peas in stew
Peas delicious
Just for you

So have a helping
To make your five
Stay really healthy
Stay alive!

Jenna Rowlands • Year 3
Eastglade Primary
Notts

My Vegetable Family

My own family are all funny 'uns
Because their favourite food is onions,
We are <u>all</u> so very healthy
Even if we're not too wealthy!
Little Lucy likes her carrots
Which make her squawk like Polly Parrot!
My daft Daddy loves his peas
But thinks they grow on giant trees
My Mummy likes her leeks for lunch
So always buys a great big bunch,
Grandad grows his own potat'ers'
Meanwhile Granny who loves all veg
Grows peppers and herbs on the window ledge.
Last of all there's me – I'm Em
And I just love everyone of them!
Veggies are our favourite food,
Come to our house, be a real cool dude!
So even if you're not that wealthy
You should still eat really healthy.

Emily Johnson • Year 4
Abbey Junior School
Darlington

Robert Pires
Footballer

Mange Toute

'Mange Toute,'
Said the French Bean
Under the Eiffel Tower.
If you eat your greens
and spinach too
You'll be strong
and full of power.

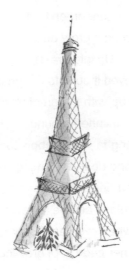

My Runner Bean
A True Story

My teacher gave me a runner bean,

Which I planted in a pot.

I wished it well as carefully

I put lots of soil on top.

Every day I watered it

And spoke gentle words to it,

And placed it in the kitchen

On a sunny sill to sit.

One day I noticed, to my delight,

Peeping through the mud,

A tiny little, pointy,

Bright green bud.

I watched it grow quite quickly,

Up into the air,

So I moved it out into the garden,

Picking it up with the greatest of care.

It curled around,

Clinging to the bamboo cane,

Soaking up the warming sun

And drinking in the rain.

I couldn't believe my eyes,

When everyday I saw

My runner bean kept growing up

More and more and more!
Then small, fat flowers appeared
And their bright colours shone,
Fiery orange and burning red,
But soon they were gone.
Then came tiny green stumps,
Hiding on delicate stems,
Looking just like
Four little green gems.
Those tiny beans grow bigger
And fatter and plumper until
Time to eat them with our Sunday roast,
Oh what a thrill!

Amber Gill • Year 5
North London Collegiate
London

Dave Crawley

Author

I Love Eating Grapes

I love eating grapes, one grape at a time
I eat them in pairs. The taste is sublime.
To bite through the skin, with juice squirting out –
That is what eating a grape is about!

I love eating grapes, I eat them in threes
In fours and in fives, they're certain to please.
More luscious than candy. More tasty than cake.
A delectable treat that I don't have to bake!

I love eating grapes. I ate the whole bunch.
So much for dessert. So, now what's for lunch?

Pineapple

Pineapple juicy,
Pineapple sweet.
Pineapple is the best fruit
I could ever eat.

Bill Payne • Year 3
Westdale Junior School
Notts

Fruit Kenning

Colour changer
Red roller
Green looker
Tooth taker
Sweet taster
Juice maker
Sun reflector
Quiet rounder
Lump maker
Soft skinner
Small pipper
Chocolate dipper
Crunchy biter
Crisp sounder

Oliver Watson • Year 3
Ranby House School
Retford, Notts

Russ Abbott
Comedian

Artichoke

It was in Jerusalem
That Arti was choking
It was for real
He wasn't joking
'Could it be the dressing?'
He did utter.
'I wish they'd serve me up with butter!'

Poem for £1

I am a little apple I'm growing on a tree

The sun and rain and wind all help to grow me.

I am red and rosy and very juicy too

I have the sweetest taste to make a pie for you.

I know someone will pick me soon and eat me for their tea

I hope another apple will grow instead of me.

Marie O'Doure-Bell • Year 3
Trinity Prep, Devon

Shakespeare's Fruit

Said Hamlet to Ophelia, 'Broccoli or Peas?
Maybe you could try some exquisite raspberries!'

Sitting on his throne, King Lear softly hummed,
'What today, hmm, I wonder, mangoes, grapes or plums?'

'Juliet,' said Romeo, 'thy beauty dost compare.
Nectarines or Sharon fruit can't match your skin so fair!'

'Ha, Ha, Ha,' cackled Lady Macbeth, 'I'll put a curse on thee,
Now, what's the magic ingredients, melons or lychees?'

Oberon and his fairies began to shout, 'Oh yey, oh yey!
All of you mere mortals should eat your five a day!!!'

Lucy Humphris • Year 6
Medstead Primary
Hampshire

Pound a Poem

If you eat broccoli cabbage and the odd aubergine it will
help to keep your waistline nice and lean!!!

But when you eat popcorn, crisps, sweets and Snickers,
you just may end up wearing BIG knickers!

Fern Liptrott • Year 5
Holy Cross RCP
St Helens.

Noah and His Ark of Fruit

One pineapple cased in armour like a fighting armadillo
Two melons each solid and spherical like a cannon ball
Three rival mangoes fresh from the sub-continent
Four russet apples plucked from Isaac Newton's garden
Five Seville oranges protected by their hardy skins
Six downy peaches each with the delicacy of a young maid
Seven kiwi fruits subtly camouflaging their
succulent interiors
Eight cherished cherries redolent of a lover's lips
Nine regal raspberries shining like crimson jewels
Ten brash bananas the admirals of the fleet
Shower upon shower of imperial grapes
Noah's amazing ark of fruit.

Henry Appleyard • Year 6
Ranby House School
Retford, Notts

Michael Lynagh

Australian Rugby Player

Game for a Peach

There it was, just out of reach,
Was it a ball or was it a peach?
Try as he could to get into this scrum
That peach was beckoning to his tum.
He touched it ... he held it
Went up and under
He dropped it again
What a blunder
He gave it a clip kick
It was rather shoddy
He charged down to the centre
Then chucked it to Noddy
'Is this my peach?' Noddy started to blubber.
'It is rather bruised, having been a grubber
But you've passed it now, you are a good chap
It's sweet, just delicious
I've won the Cap.'

The Raspberry

I look at it.
It looks like pink frog spawn
Without the tadpoles.

It smells like fresh spring air
On a wet, foggy morning.

It feels like soft clouds
Drifting in the sky.

When I eat it,
I suck it to get all the juice out.

My raspberry tastes like melting marshmallows
Dribbling down my chin.

sshlupp!

Martha Hitchin • Year 3
Trinity Primary School
Hereford

Superman Grape Returns

Superman grape wears a red and blue cape,
And soars over houses and rooves,
Then he lands on the ground without making a sound
And gets squished under horses' hooves!

Grapey visits heaven at five minutes to seven,
He's purple and shiny and smooth.

His house is a fruit bowl,
A bottomless dark hole,
And he lives with bananas and cherries.
He's small and smooth and delicious and round,
He is purple and pinky and looks like a berry.

Cecilia Hobbs • Year 4
Boughton Under Bleam Primary
Faversham

Reasons to Eat Fruit and Veg

If you eat too much cake, you will be sick
for heaven's sake.

And if you eat veg one, two, three, people grow healthy
as you see.

Cancer is a nasty disease so try to eat fruit and
veg please.

William Penn •Year 3
Read School, Selby

Pomegranate

Each seed is a ruby ready to burst.
A jewel with a secret to share.
A scarlet drop of passion.
A swallow of sweetness.
A crystal of syrup.
A pippy flower of gems.
Sweet but bitter,
Bitter but sweet.
A confusion of tastes.

Lucy Lewis • Year 5
Maunden Primary
Herts

Darcey Bussell CBE
Prima Ballerina

Nutcracker

To crack a nut
Is a festive treat
With oranges and figs
Which taste so sweet
With plums and grapes
Which taste so fine
And cranberries and currants
What a wonderful time!

Off To Pick Some Fruit And Veg

Out of the car, I can almost breathe in the taste of fruit
First to the strawberries, wonderfully juicy, squished and
pressed between happy fingers,
Boys and girls chase each other through the hedges,
raspberries clamouring to be eaten on every branch,
Sombre blackberries, sharp when bitten from the top,
but when taken from the bottom wonderously sweet,
Beans huddled in groups, whispering together on
the hard earth floor,
Peas in their pods, hiding under the leaves, determined
never to be found,
Carrots struggling to stay underground, too tired to come out,
Tall golden corn, escaping the dull life below and rising to
the heavens above.

I walk out of the curling lettuce patch, feel the earth
underneath my feet, see the cornflower blue sky overhead
and look down at my baskets, some filled with fruit, some
filled with vegetables, but all of them
filled with anticipation.

Imogen Edwards–Lawrence • Year 4
Putney High School, London

Lost Tomato

I'm a tomato, but I'm very sad.
I don't know what to do, this is bad.
I have no friends. Why? I don't know.
Maybe it's because I'm a tomato.

I don't know whether to hang out with my old chums:
The apples, bananas, peaches and plums.
Or should I be with my buds:
The carrots, the celery, the broccoli and spuds.

The reason why I'm so confused
Is because I feel I'm being used.
I don't know if I should hang with the fruit or veg.
I'm a tomato! Just call me a 'freg'!

Anne-Marie Ikegwuru • Year 6
Brunswick Park Primary School
London

The Dragon Fruit

Inside the fiery spikes is the scorching beach,
Inside the scorching beach is the black eye,
Inside the black eye is the hot sand,
Inside the hot sand is the white inside
Inside the white inside is the tropical breeze,
Inside the tropical breeze is the black stone,
Inside the black stone are the swaying trees,
Inside the swaying trees are the crimson spikes,
Inside the crimson spikes is the tropical ocean,
Inside the tropical ocean is the dark eye,
Inside the dark eye is the swaying in the wind,
Inside the swaying in the wind are the fiery spikes.

Rem Coppock-Cudd • Year 5
Cokethorpe School
Oxfordshire

Sam Stern

Chef

How to Make a Strawberry Smoothie

Take...

1 banana (peeled and chopped)
A few washed blueberries
A few chopped, washed strawberries

Stick...

The lot in a blender or a plastic jug

Drizzle...

A bit of lovely honey in there

Pour...

Milk over the lot. Half a pint or so.

Or…

Sub plain or vanilla yoghurt for some of the milk

Blitz

in your blender

Or…

use a handblender in your jug

Sip it…

Through a straw

Or…..

Just drink it

For

Breakfast,lunch, after school

Whenever

The Pumpkin

I'm an enormous pumpkin,
I grew in Edward's plot.
In the October sunshine,
I shine orange and hot.
I won first prize in Potters Bar,
The biggest veggie there,
I am the proudest pumpkin,
Because of Edward's care.
At Halloween my tummy's scraped,
Eyes, nose and mouth cut neat.
My candle burns so hot inside,
I'm off to trick or treat.

Boo!

Edward Dutton • Year 3
Manor Lodge School
Hertfordshire

Jacqueline Wilson

Author and Former Children's Laureate

Apple

I walk beside the Fairfield
And on past Orchard Way
The names are faint reminders
When the countryside
held sway

The town spreads out behind me
Many multi-stories steep
McDonalds in the market place
Instead of cows and sheep

Down the park to my house
That's twice as old as me
Unlatch the garden gate
And stand beneath my tree

Its gnarled old branches laden
With apples, tart and green
The last tree of that orchard
When Victoria was Queen

I pick an apple from a twig
And cup it in my hand
So glad a little countryside
Is still here on my land.

Eric Ode

Songwriter, Author, Poet, Musical Kids' Entertainer

Tossed Salad

I tosesd me a salad
as fien as you plaes
with carorts and cabbage
and pepeprs and peas

I threw on soem pikcels,
one swete and oen suor,
some raidshes,riasnis,
and ripe caluilfwore

I cleaned a cuuccmber
and gaev it a chop.
I tosesd in a turnip
but still coudlt'n stpo.

I added some olvies
and oonins for fun.
I strired in some spniach
but still wans't doen.

I lokoed all aruond,
and I bet you cna tell,
I pikced up thsi poem
and tosesd it as wlel.

Raspberries

Their hairy bumpy shapes glimmer in the sunlight
The allotments are teeming with people
A woman arrives, comes over, stoops to pick
the raspberries.
One by one they are dropped in a large brown basket
They jostle each other as they tumble downwards
Into the bottom of the basket.
Suddenly they are upturned into a cool white bowl
The woman brings out a spoon and she
starts to crush them.
Raspberry juices spurt everywhere – bright as blood
The bruised bodies of the raspberries float
amongst scarlet juices.
Gingerly, she lays them on a table
And soon the bowl is empty.

Peter Hart • Year 6
Fosse Bank School
Kent

The Fruity Beach

I see the sun glowing like a tanned orange,
Starfish fading as I eat my star fruit,
Seaweed washed up like rambutan;
Boys standing with spiked hair like pineapples,
Undressed boats floating like unpeeled bananas.
I feel the wind like shadows of fruit and
veg gracefully gliding into a salad.
Stones, still and silent like apples in a bowl;
Creative burrowing crabs trying to get
away from my powerful tomato.
My fruit eaten,
The beach swallowed by darkness.

Jasmin Boomer • Year 5
Birdham Primary School
West Sussex

Maureen Lipman

Actor, author and poet

Veggie Tables and Fruit Machinations

A beetroot's a neat root
A grapefruit's a great fruit
A potato is bolder
With a chip on its shoulder

A tomato frittata
Is good for a starter
If beanz meanz Heinz
Grapes meanz vines

Green beans, broad beans, haricot verts
String beans, mung beans, flageolet rare
Watch for the wind in globe artichokes
Not everyone relishes low farty jokes

Plus leeks and asparagus
Also embarrass us
And frankly, there's a few carbs
In healthy young rhubarbs

Downtown Abu Dhabi
They're mad for kohlrabi
But seldom would falsify
Their loathing for salsify

Mulberries, bilberries, cherries and guavas
Blueberries, raspberries, small green bananas
Tangerine, mandarin, kumquats, satsumas
Pineapple's good for the throat, I've heard rumours

I'm pink therefore I'm yam
Here's plums in your jam
How swede it all looks
'A turnip for the books'

I've long been a buyer
Of fleshy papaya
And often dice celery
In a manner Nigella-ry

Spinach and broccoli diced rather choppily
Radish and rocket leaf, that's eating properly!
Five fruits 'n' veg daily, try not to miss them
They'll pull antioxidants into your system!

Auntie Sarah's Garden

Hey Mr Frog what can you see?
Can you see some sweetcorn as tall as me?

Hey Mr Bird flying over head
Can you see some lettuce lying in the bed?

Hey Mr Rabbit hopping about
Can you see some carrots popping out?

Hey Mr Worm wriggling in the soil
Can you see some beetroot ready to boil?

Hey all the animals what can you see?
A garden full of vegetables for you and for me!

Madeleine Hill • Year 3
Great Alne Primary School,
Alcester, Warwickshire

Scoot and Reg

There were two brothers Scoot and Reg
Who argued over fruit and veg
Scoot said that fruit would build your muscles
While Reg raved on about green brussels

He said that peas fresh from the pod
Would guarantee a healthy bod
But Scoot said no fruit tastes the best
Ok said Reg we'll have a test

Each prepared their favourite treat
And gave each other this to eat
This tastes fantastic declared Scoot
As he ate up the veggie soup

Well said Reg I must admit
This fresh fruit salad did the trick
So Scoot and Reg now do agree
That they can both eat sensibly.

Joey Tucker • Year 6
Lipson Vale Primary,
Devon

Matthew Fitt
Poet

Mr Moncrieff the Greengrocer's song

(Tune the banana boat song)

Aipples,ai-ai-ai aipples
Gloamin comes
And I want tae go hame

Tatties, a- ah-ah –ah atties,
Gloamin comes
And I wanna go hame.

No wan, no twa, but three big tumshies
Pit them in a poke
And jist let me go hame.

Ingans, I say ing I say ing
Il say ih ih ingans
Gloamin comes
And I want tae go hame.

I sell neeps and kail and hinnie-bobbies
I'm seik o it aw
And I wanna go hame.

Brammles, I say bram, I say bram,
I say bram, I say bram, I say brah-ah-ammles
Gie me a punnet
And I'm gaun hame too.

Konnie Huq

Television Presenter

When Feeling Glum …

When feeling glum
I eat a plum
When dancing the tango
I chew on a mango
Oranges are nice
When giving advice
And strawberries are sweet
With cream, they're a treat
But when I'm feeling really blue
Nothing but a banana will do

Linda Knauss

Poet

Caesar Salad

The lettuce turned its leafy head
Tomatoes couldn't bare it.
The beets had blushed their deepest red
and hid behind a carrot.

I can't say why (they never talked)
And so I'm only guessing.
But maybe vegetables are shocked
When they see Caesar dressing.

Should I Eat Vegetables?

'Should I eat vegetables?' I heard my friend say,
'Do I really need to eat my five a day?
Isn't fruit for grown ups? It doesn't taste very nice,
I like my sweets – like chocolate mice.'

If you don't want pains in your wrists and knees,
Then you should eat plenty of carrots and peas.
If you want a lean body with good, strong muscles,
Then you should eat plenty of Brussels.
Vegetables are good for you in more than one way,
They do help us all to think and to play.
With different tastes and textures too,
Sure fruit and veg are good for you!
They have different colours as you will see,
The answer to your question will have to be,
If you want to be healthy and stay alive
Then try and eat your daily five!

Daniel Greenwood • Year 5
Grange Primary School
Notts

The Banana

On the outside
It's like a newly printed book
Waiting for you to pick it up, open it,
And enjoy its soft, silky pages.

It is shaped like a boat,
Bobbing on a peacefully flowing stream,
Floating dreamily across the twinkling waters.

It is a luminous yellow,
As if it had just been newly painted,
Tempting as it sits in the fruit bowl.

It is soft and sweet on the inside,
And you can mash it if you wish,
It's sometimes stringy like a spider's newly made web.

It is sweet, when you slice it with your teeth,
It lights up your mouth,
As if you have just swallowed a sunbeam.

Laura Gathercole • Year 5
St Mary's School
Colchester

Clayton Blackmore
Former Footballer

Pak to Noodle

We're going to Pak
Said Noodle to Choi
Is it for real
Or is it a ploy

Are we going to have
A nasty shock
As our destination
Could be the Wok!

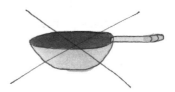

The Pear

As the heavenly fruit sits and waits,
To be cut open and have its crisp, ripe flesh
Swallowed and crunched,
Right down to the centre.
My mind drifts to a late autumn evening,
In an English country orchard,
The branches and leaves dappled.
Dappled with golden sunlight,
The last before the winter frost.
Not a movement to be seen
Until suddenly, the late, gentle breeze
Sweeps a juicy, bulging fruit from its place
on the tree,
It dances as it falls,
Falling softly onto a bed of golden leaves.
Its green perfect, yet imperfect shape
Nestling in the rustle of nature.

Lucy Holden • Year 6
North London Collegiate

Anthony Horowitz

Author

Cauliflower

Vegetables are good for you
They say and it may well be true
But there's a vegetable I hate
So much that if it's on my plate
I'll run away and not come back
Or fake a massive heart attack
The cauliflower's what I mean
That nasty white and pale green!
So soft and lumpy on the tongue
It tastes (and feels) a bit like dung.
If boiled up and then served plain
It looks just like a human brain
But worse are all those recipes
That try to smother it in cheese
My mum once cooked it, I recall –
It wasn't a success at all

The guests, by chance, were Japanese
She served them cauliflower cheese
And though they'd all been bright and cheery
They committed *Hari Kiri*
Plunging swords into their chests
So typical of foreign guests!
But all of them had had enough –
They couldn't bear to eat the stuff
And as I listened to their cries
What could I do but sympathise?
Say what you like, but as for me
I don't care if its blasphemy –
God didn't have his finest hour
When He created cauliflower.

Tatties

Mash 'em

Munch 'em

Crisp 'em

Crunch 'em

Boil 'em

Bake 'em

Fluff 'em

Flake 'em

Rinse 'em

Roast 'em

Taste 'em

Toast 'em

Halve 'em

Heat 'em

Like 'em

Eat 'em!!

Rhona MacKillop • Year 6
The Mary Eskine & Stewart's Melville Junior School
Edinburgh

Lester Headley

Poet

Tomato and I

Plant me from my seedlings in any turf or cut down old pail
When I am you call me tomato when I am with my cousins
you call me tomatoes
Round or oblong am I but often I grow like a ball
I am red and inside I have seeds, water and all
I can add beauty upon your dinner plate.

You can eat me anytime early or late
I am loved by many chefs slim, fat, short or tall
Place me inside your fridge
Eat of me every day
I will contribute to your daily health care.

Three Cheers for Vegetables

Well, if you're asking me,
Vegetables are just great,
So many to choose from,
And I pile them on my plate.

They come in lots of colours,
The choice is very good,
They're packed with vitamins and minerals,
They're really healthy food.

My favourite is the potato,
I eat them every day,
Baked, roasted, boiled or mashed,
Every day a different way.

So if you want to be healthy,
And feel and do your best,
Then just eat lots of vegetables
Drink water, and get your rest.

They really are all natural,
Well, they do grow in the ground,
No additives or colourings,
No preservatives to be found.

So grab your fork, and get stuck in,
What more can I say?
Pile your plate, then ask for more,
Make this a 'veggie day'.

But, to all you people reading this,
Who think I've gone quite mad,
I do agree with all of you,
Who say spinach tastes real bad!

Alasdair Wright • Year 5
Hexham Middle School

Paul Robinson
England and Tottenham Hotspur Goalkeeper

Parsley and Dill

Parsley and Dill
Grew up on the Hill
With Mustard Cress and Water
Parsley was flaked
And Dill got baked
And Rosemary fell down
With laughter.

Michaela Morgan

Author

Fruit Loopy

You can juggle it, you can juice it.

You can squish and you can squoosh it.

If you're batty as a bat, you could wear it as a hat. You can
pick it, you can pack it

in the pocket of your jacket.

If you're feeling cool and groovy

you can eat it as a smoothie.

You can suck or you can crunch lots.

You can take it in your lunch box.

You can put it in a jelly – any way you fill your belly.

You can chop it, you can chill it,

Oh just get a bowl and fill it.

Slice it in a glass – and cheers!

Wear some cherries on your ears.

You can mash it, you can mix it.
You can eat it in a biscuit.
You can bake it or milkshake it – any way you
want to take it.
Share it with a load of llamas
Why not? Just go BANANAS!
Fruit – you cannot beat it
… So just EAT IT!

The Apple

Look at me…
What do you see?

I can be green
or red.

I have a stalk
that cannot talk.

I roll like a ball
but I'm not spotted at all.

I am round like a pound
but I can't make a sound.

I'm munchy and crunchy
and tasty to eat.

I've a seed in the core
but not any more.

Soon you may see
what I may be.

I am picked off a tree
but ripe I may be.

What am I?
I am an apple.

Chloe Baxter • Year 4
Bognall Primary School
West Lothian

The Coconut

The nut-brown, solid coconut,
Size of a small, hairy rugby ball,
Fresh from an exotic palm tree somewhere on a desert island,
Drifted on the crest of the waves on the deep, blue,
sparkling sea.

Like a giant's teardrop, only solid and nut coloured,
Mouth watering, sweet milk, hiding away inside the shell –
like prison,
As it soothes my tastebuds it's like being on a rollercoaster
as it falls down into my tummy,
All I can say is YUMMY, YUMMY, YUMMY!

As the rock is thrown to break the shell pure, white flesh
jumps out of it,
All that is left is like a shattered piece of china on the floor,
I pick up a broken piece of milky, white flesh,
Gulp it down, incredibly fresh
Flesh so sweet it could be a Bounty itself.

Gone forever now.

Genevieve Braund • Year 5
Tickhill Estfield Primary
South Yorkshire

Francesca Simon

Children's Author

Beans

I don't write poems but this is Henry's favourite …

Beans, beans, good for the heart
The more you eat, the more you …

Kenn Nesbitt
Poet

Crazy over Veg

I tasted some asparagus
What scrupulous little spears!
I kept on eating corn until
It came out of my ears

So now I'm eating artichokes
And radishes and peas
I've gone completely loony
Over vegetables like these

I'm going crazy
It's crazy but its true
I'm crazy over vegetables
I love them, yes I do

I'm going crazy
Try some and you'll see
That you'll be going crazy
Over vegetables like me

I'm going crazy
That's how I want to be
I hope that some day everyone
Is crazy just like me.

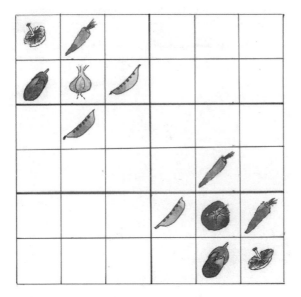

Ted Scheu

Children's Poet

Turn The Spoon Over Dear

A kid from the city of York
Could only eat peas with a fork,
One Sunday at noon he tried using a spoon,
But he could never get it to work.

Vegetable Scream

You may have them every day,
You will have them every meal,
But have you ever wondered
How vegetables really feel?

Have you listened carefully
to a carrot scream and squeal
as your mum grates so carefully
and serves it with your meal!

What about potatoes
as you chop them into fries
as you boil them or you mash them
have you ever heard their cries?

So mum, as you nag me daily
to eat the stuff that's green
it's not that I'm unhealthy,
it's you that's being mean!

William Samuels • Year 4
Manor Lodge School
Hertfordshire

Diana Hendry

Author and Poet

Potato Cuts

This is not potato country. Rice
Long grain short brown white
Basmati, Uncle Ben's – and pasta –
Spaghetti, vermicelli, tagliatelli, but
potatoes no. Only one thing's passing as spuds
sweating and sprouting in sticky plastic

There are losses one learns to live with. Horses and carts,
a health service, lovers, clean streets.
Justice, an empire – possibly tobacco
But potatoes no.
Which is why I have
grown this terrible nostalgia for the earlies;

For that secret moment in the allotment
When we forked them up archaeologically
Jubilant, for those Sunday jaunts
With the kids in the fields

For my mother mashing and boiling entirely without
reverence for Sunday's roasts; for Springs
butter and parsley,
For grandad's chip butties. Oh for all
the tangled roots and attachments
just under the surface of unreachable childhood.

HOME
GROWN
POTATOES

Bob Willis
Former England Cricketer

Greens

There was a cricket on the pitch
Who dreamed of eating greens
He was the biggest cricket
That you have ever seen

He had a bumper appetite
And took off for a spin
He munched and munched his googly greens
So he was never thin.

Richard Phillips
Radio Presenter

Forbidden Love

Once there was a plum
Who loved beyond his reach
For he yearned not for
Another plum,
But for the sweetest peach.

And the peach loved him back
With ardour just as strong,
Though she knew she should
Turn away
That their love was wrong.

Their parents tried to reason
Peaches weren't meant for plums.
Why must they take this
Fateful course?
Could they not just be chums?

'Oh plummie' said she sobbing,
'This just cannot be done.'
But insisted he,

'Courage ma pêche.
Our flesh shall soon be one.'

He cried 'I won't give up,
I'd be dead just as soon.
I won't let passion
Wither 'til
I'm a dried up prune.'

And so these star-crossed lovers
One night they did cross genes,
And soon they had a
Family of
The cutest nectarines.

The Fruit Bowl

We all wait in the fruit bowl hoping to get picked.

The big yellow smooth banana,

The round juicy green apple

The soft fat pear

The tiny sweet grape

The squashy red raspberry

They all chatter about getting picked.

'I hope it's me' said the fat pear

'I think it's going to be me' said the big yellow
smooth banana.

Then they all go quiet as the huge hand grabs
the tiny sweet grape,

Oh well they all sigh, maybe next time.

Jenni Sheridan • Year 3
Kings Hill School
Kent

The Fruit Party

I love to tango with a mango
It's fruity and it's fun.
I like the way it moves and sways,
But it's not the only one!

I love to be merry with any berry,
They're juicy and so sweet.
But watch out where you dance around,
They leave stains upon your feet.

I love to make shapes with grapes.
They jiggle and they jive.
But most of all, I love all fruit,
It makes me feel alive.

Isabel Flynn • Year 3
Tillingbourne Junior School
Surrey

Robert Pottle

Children's Poet

My Brother Will Not Eat His Veggies

My brother will not eat his veggies
He eats mostly unhealthy food
I think that it might be his diet
That makes him so terribly rude.

For breakfast he likes to eat pastries
He then wipes his hands on his shirt
He burps and he won't say 'Excuse me'
Instead he demands his dessert.

Me I prefer veggie omlettes
With peppers, tomatoes and cheese
I eat with my very best manners,
And always say thank you and please.

I wish that my brother ate veggies
I think that is all it would take
To make him a well mannered brother,
But he just eats candy and cake.

Last night I was eating my carrots
He grabbed one and gave it a try.
I watched his reaction and noticed
A strange look came into his eye.

Were vegetables giving him manners,
Or would he remain rude and curt?
My question was answered the second
he burped and asked, 'Where's my dessert?'

I haven't lost faith in my veggies.
They do make you healthy and bright.
Their powers are truly amazing,
But they can't make your brother polite.

Fab Fruit Salad

Mad Melon's wife was a Crazy Coconut,
They were ever so happy and cheery but...
Everybody laughed at the odd looking 'pear'
It almost squeezed both to the edge of despair!

Bonkers Banana said they'd definitely 'split',
Two different fruit, they just didn't fit.
Perfect Peach said they would never last,
And the Strawberry Field was simply aghast.

But as we all know,
Seeds of love grow.
Skin doesn't matter when inside is kind,
We can all find sweetness under the rind.

Jessica Veysey • Year 4
Glyncoed Junior School
Cardiff

The Satsuma Samba

This is a special time of year,
The ultimate dancing bananza.

When all the coolest fruit in town,
Go to the Satsuma Samba.

The paparazzi are all over the place,
To see the cool fruit dance-a

'Cause all the poshest fruit in town
head to the Satsuma Samba.

Lemon-Em and his cool band,
The amazing wicked rapper

He'll be there for all the fans
At the Satsuma Samba.

Come on, head down with us tonight,
The music's gonna rock-a!

We will go there with you tonight,
To the Satsuma Samba.

James Barton • Year 5
Eglwys Wen Primary School
Whitchurch, Cardiff

The Tale of the Lovesick Carrot

There once was a carrot,
Who fell in love with a parrot.
But the parrot loved a mango,
Who was always drunk on Tango.
But the mango loved a plum,
Who lived with his mum.
So some fruits love each other,
And some live with their mother.

Kirsten McPhail • Year 6
Our Lady Queen of Martyrs School
Durham

Darren Sardelli
Children's Author

Cupid's Arrow

When I was in the lunchroom,
Eating cherry pie
Cupid shot an arrow
That hit me in the thigh.

I looked up at the ceiling
And saw him with his bow
He took another arrow
And shot me in the toe.

A jolt went through my body
And knocked me off my seat.
I felt a happy tingle,
Which made me shake my feet.

I landed on an apple
The apple looked so cute,
I simply cannot help it,
I am now in love with FRUIT!

Which one are you?

If I were a cabbage,
I'd be all heart!
If I were a baked bean,
I might make you fart!
If I were a carrot
I'd see well at night!
If I were a prickly pear,
I'd give you a fright!
If I were a runner bean,
I'd be quick off the plate!
If I were a jacket spud,
I'd choose cheese for a mate!
If I were an orange,
I'd be juicy and so sweet!
If I were a strawberry,
I'd look good enough to eat!
If I were an onion,
I'm bound to make you cry!
If I were a pepper,
I'd go well with stir fry!
If I were a banana,
I could give you the slip!
If I were a pomegranate,
You'd really get the pip!
If I were a chilli,
I'd hot things up a bit!
If I were a cucumber,
I'd get rid of that zit!
If I were a lemon,

I'd fill you with zest!
If I were a Bramley apple,
My crumble is the best!
If I were a green grape,
I'd make a nice sweet wine!
If I were a small green pea,
Out of pod, is out of line!

If you were a fruit or veg,
Which one would you be?
Apricot, cauliflower
Or a stick of celery?

Lauren Gregory • Year 6
Lightwood's Primary School

Who Am I?

I'm green and hairy
And shaped like an egg.
When you fancy a sweet,
Have me instead.
I'll tickle your taste buds.
I'm full of vitamin C
Have you guessed what I am yet?

I'm a Kiwi!

YIPPEE!

Kelsey Jones • Year 3
Walmley Junior School
West Midlands

Diana Moran

'Green Goddess' – Fitness Expert and Journalist

An Apple a Day

An apple a day keeps the doctor away
Or so they say …
A vegetable a day helps you work, rest and play
Is what I say.
Five fresh fruits and vegetables too
Eaten each day are so good for you
They'll help you to grow and make you strong
So eat lots today and you won't go wrong!

The Ugly Fruit

I accompany my mother down the supermarket aisles
I see shiny red apples, bananas in piles
The same old thing in the same old place
But then something catches my eye and this isn't the
case It's nobbly and bobbly and it most certainly
lives up to its name
Ladies and Gentlemen please put your hands
together for the 'Ugly Fruit!'
I persuade my mum to please let me try
With a huff and a puff she agrees to buy
I cannot wait to get home, my impatience
I swear you can touch
I believe I can taste it, it's all getting too much
Then we finally get home, I scramble through the bags
My mother gets cross and begins with the nags
Then there I see it next to the beans and ham

I grab the knife, peel, slice and wham
Finally the fruit is melting in my mouth
As I chew and ponder and it slowly heads south
Now I decide I have to declare
The moral of this poem I have to prepare
Please don't judge a book by it's cover
There are special things to be found if you spend
time to uncover.

Zak Pinder • Year 5
Tottington Primary
Lancashire

Sarah Midda

Author

Potato to Leek

Said the potato to the leek, when shall we meet?

With the meat

In the soup or the salad

On pasta or rice

Baked, then a slice or two,

On toast or in stew

With all the others, their vegetable brothers,

Or sisters or cousins, or whatever relation

To cause both culinary and healthy sensation.

Fiona Bruce

Newsreader and Presenter

Eat Your Veg

Don't want lettuce,
Do like beans,
Never cabbage,
Might eat greens,
Love my peas,
Broccoli and corn,
Eat your veg,
From dusk til dawn,
Don't delay, don't you wait,
Get some veg upon your plate.

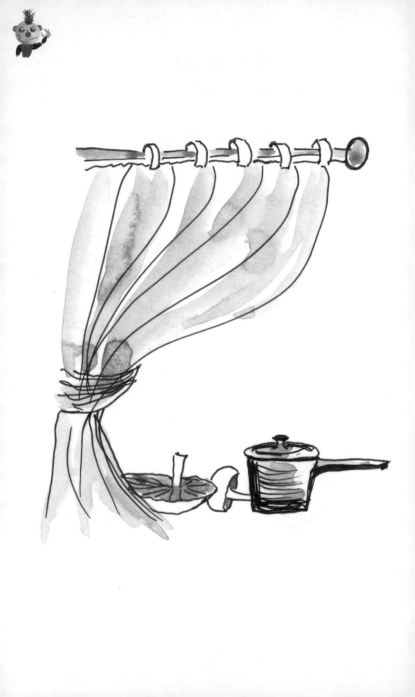

Gervase Phinn

Author

Dominic's Discovery

She secretes them in spaghetti
Hides them under chips
Camouflages them in pizza
Buries them in dips.
She wraps them up in batter
Conceals them in baked beans
Envelops them in gravy
Disperses them in greens.
She chops them up with onions
Sprinkles them with cheese
Mashes them with cabbage
Scatters them in peas.
She covers them in ketchup
Submerges them in stew
But he can still taste mushrooms
Whatever mum tries to do.

Andrea Shavick

Author and Poet

What Made You So Clever?

Fruit makes you clever
Stimulates the brain
Eat fruit and you'll never
Be the same again

Can't play that Grade 1 piece?
You'll whiz up to 8
Can't get to class on time?
With fruit you'll never be late

Don't know how to spell long words?
You will if do as I say
Even Algebra's easy
On five portions a day

But just one word of warning
NEVER tell a soul
NOBODY needs to know it was fruit
That made you score all those goals

So when your friends come asking
'What made your IQ soar?'
Just tell them you were hit on the head
By a meteor

The Fruit Stall Ball

The fruit stall in the evening
When the lights have all gone out
Is a party for the peaches
Who often scream and shout!

When every single mango
Wears a party hat
And the plums all do the tango,
Then start cheering just like that!

When the grapes are all a-groovin'
And the blood red cherries dance
The blackberries aren't moving
They're just standing in a trance.

There's a time for peaceful music
But for now it's rock 'n' roll
There's a time for blues and opera
And for hip-hop and for soul.

There's a rock band of bananas
With sunglasses and all
This is MIDNIGHT MAYHEM
At the funky fruit stall!!

I can assure you, no fruit's feelings were hurt in
the making of this poem...

Alice Singleton • Year 6
Woodchester Endowed Primary

Graeme Souness
Former Footballer and Manager

Apple Ball

Round hard and shiny, lined up in rows
Waiting to be chosen, which one, who knows?

Will it be her, or will it be him?
Braeburn, Pink Lady or Cox's Pippin?

Slice, chop, grate, quarter and stew,
Bake, crumble, puff, so much they can do.

But when Eve tempted Adam, it was no good at all.
Was that the first apple or the first football?

Graham Denton

Poet

How Un-Appletising!

We never ask my Dad to cook –
There wouldn't be that much to eat;
He thinks, to make an apple puff,
You chase an apple up the street!

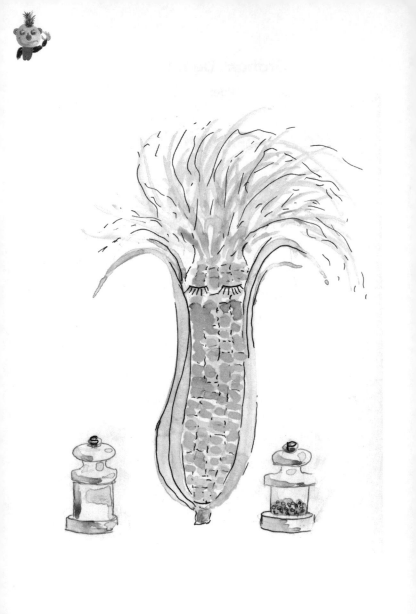

Johnny Briggs
Actor

Corn on The Cob

What a good job
Said Corn on the Cob
His lashes all of a flutter
With Pepper and Salt
That's how we've been taught
To eat him with melted butter!

When I Close My Eyes

If someone asked what I prefer,
A juicy apple or a firm pear,
I would close my eyes and think very hard
And dream of the lovely apple yard,
And when I close my eyes again,
I'll think of pear trees in the rain.

If I was asked another time,
To pick a favourite veg of mine,
My eyes would close, and there I'd see,
Swede and parsnips waiting for me,
With carrots and peas and onions too
Mixed up together in a tasty stew.

If one last time I was asked to choose,
Between fruit and veg, the fruit would lose,
Because every time my eyelids shut,
I always think of Sunday lunch,
Roast beef and vegetables on my plate,
Can't stop, must go, don't want to be late.

Alex Bradley • Year 5
Walmley Junior School
West Midlands

Sheena Blackhall

Writer

The Denner Wifie's Girn

I chap fruit an vegg fur schule denner
Avocada an aiupple an pear
I chap them perjink or squeeze inno a drink
The bree frae an orange, wi care

As I wyle an wash an I peel them
I mynd upon derk Halloween
As a littlin I dookit fur aipples
An howkit oot neep lantern een

Syne I dice up the kail an the cabbage
Pare tattie an carrot an ingin
Kennin fine fin the bairns see the broth pot
They'll cry oot 'Gad's sake' or 'Thon's mingin'

The bell brings them in wi a rummle
There's dirdin an clunkin o plate
I staun at the back o the veggies
An serve baith the cauld as the hett

'I dinna wint greens, they're jist boggin,'
Says loon wi a facefu o plooks
An a quine girns 'I'm nae ettin ingins
They'll connach ma braith. Ingin sooks!'

Syne I teem oot the veg in the backet
Healthy menus are affa sair wark
I telt ae wee bairn, 'Ett yer carrots
Anye'll get tae see in the derk'

He tried his first carrot this denner
'They're crunchy an tasty' quo he
A convert tae fresh fruit and veggie
An miracle wiker wis me!

He scored twenty goals in the playgrun
Star striker without ony doot
'Fits the secret?' the ither bairns winnert
An he skirled oot 'It's veggies and fruit'

Apples

My mum and dad they always nag,
Eat an apple it's good for you lad.
Green or red it really doesn't matter,
An apple a day will never make you fatter,
The doctor and dentist you will never see,
As long as you eat as many as me,
Coxes, Granny Smiths or Golden Delicious,
They taste just great and are really nutritious.

Joseph Savage-Crieghton • Year 6
Farnham Common Junior
Buckinghamshire

Celia Abrahams

The Seed Was Sewn

The seed was sewn
The idea was planted
Pound a Poem was born....
It was enchanted

This was a dream
Could it come true?
It could only happen
Through all of you

The plan was plotted
It started to grow
It was fed and nurtured
The fruit started to show

Each leaf that sprouted
Encouraged the growth
Literacy and charity
We could have both

We added some fun
To the taste of fruit
An ode to a plum
Would be rather cute

Kids must eat veg
We all agreed
How can we make them?
Beg and Plead?

No …. a Rhyme, a creation
That they could enjoy
Make it funny or whacky
For each girl and boy

The place to hold this
Has to be school
Let's make it trendy
Let's make it cool

It's grown now … fertile
Ripe and ready to flourish
For their minds, their bodies
And their souls to nourish

There's a gratitude that's grown
Born of confidence and belief
In this concept that's now
Much more than a leaf

It's a fully grown tree
That has burst into bloom
Thanks to all in these leaves
Excitement will loom

You have encouraged… and been
Incredibly staunch,
And now it's arrived
Pound a Poem's book launch

No, it won't be the last
And we want you to know
Next year's Pound a Poem
Will certainly grow

To encourage these children
To write us a rhyme
Entering Pound a Poem
They'll have good time

Pound a Poem endorses,
Please take our tip,
Healthy eating
Literacy, citizenship

The Winners

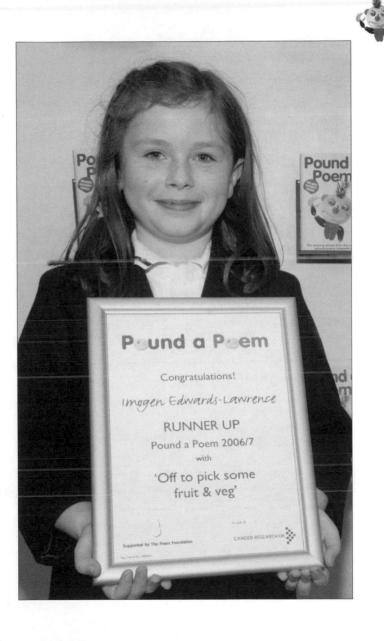

Annabel Karmel's Fruit Smoothies

A good way to include more fruit in your diet is to make fruit smoothies. These are fun for children to make themselves and they can experiment with making their own combinations.

Strawberries and Cream

1 medium banana, peeled and cut into chunks
1 handful/5 to 8 medium-sized 90g/3 oz strawberries,
hulled and halved
½ of a 170g/6 oz pot of strawberry yoghurt
60 ml/4 tbsp cream soda

Put the banana, strawberries and yoghurt into a blender and whiz for 1 to 2 minutes, until smooth. Add cream soda and whiz again until frothy. Pour into a glass to serve.

Makes one glass

Sunshine Smoothie

1 medium banana, peeled and cut into chunks

1 handful mango chunks (100g)

1 tsp honey

120 ml pineapple juice

4 tbsp orange juice

Put the banana, mango and honey into a blender and whiz for 1 to 2 minutes until smooth. Add the pineapple and orange juice and whiz again, until frothy. Pour into a glass to serve.

Makes one glass

Peach Melba

75g fresh raspberries
half x 425g can peach slices or 2 sweet ripe peaches
200 ml raspberry drinking yoghurt
100 ml milk
1 tbsp icing sugar (or to taste)

Puree together the raspberries and peaches and push through a sieve to remove the seeds. Using a hand blender, blend the yoghurt, fruits milk and icing sugar until smooth.

Makes two glasses

Recipes from Annabel Karmel's *Favourite Family Recipes* published by Ebury.
Reprinted by kind permission of the Random House Group Ltd.

About Cancer Research UK

Cancer Research UK is the world's leading independent organisation dedicated to cancer research.

With an annual scientific spend of £257 million, we fund over 3,000 world-class scientists, doctors and nurses in England, Scotland, Wales and Northern Ireland. Their combined expertise puts us at the forefront of cancer research. Indeed, we were recently ranked among the top three biomedical research organisations in the world.

We fund an extensive programme of cancer research in hospitals, institutes and universities in over 35 cities and towns across the UK. We probably fund a scientist near you!

CHILDREN'S CANCERS

Cancer Research UK is proud to be a major funder of children's cancer research in the UK, where more than 7 out of 10 children with cancer are now successfully treated, compared to fewer than 3 in 10 during the 1960s. Improvements in survival are largely due to large, international clinical trials of treatments for children's cancer, many of which are co-ordinated in the UK. Proceeds from this book will help to support the charity's vital research into children's cancer.

Thank you for your support.
Together we will beat cancer.

www.visitbarbados.co.uk

Pound a Poem and Cancer Research UK would like to thank the Barbados Tourism Authority for their generosity and support in donating the wonderful first prize to the competition.

To find out more about the work of Cancer Research UK and details of the 2008 Pound a Poem competition log on to:

www.cancerresearchuk.org